MW00416676

The First Transcontinental Railroad

A History of the Building of the Pacific Railroad

By James K. Wheaton

Golgotha Press

www.golgothapress.com

Table of Contents

Error! Not a valid heading level range.

Introduction

The First Transcontinental Railroad, originally called the Pacific Railroad, was a railroad built in the United States between 1863 and 1869 that connected the western part of America with its eastern part. Built by the Central Pacific Railroad of California and the Union Pacific Railroad, it connected the Eastern terminus of Council Bluffs, Iowa/Omaha, Nebraska with the railroad lines of the Pacific Ocean at Oakland, California. In time, it would link in with the existing railway network present on the Eastern Coast of America, thus connecting the Atlantic and Pacific coast of the United States for the first time by rail. Because of this, the line received a second nickname, "the Overland Route."

The railroad was a government operation, authorized by Congress during the height of the Civil War. Congress passed the Pacific Railroad Acts in 1862 and again in 1864. To pay for it, the US government issued 30 year bonds, as well as granting government land to contractors. The construction of the line was a major achievement by both the Union Pacific (constructing westward from Iowa) and the Central Pacific (constructing eastward from California). The line was officially opened on May 10, 1869, with the Last Spike driven through the railway at Promontory Summit, Utah.

The Transcontinental Railroad revolutionized

both the population and economy of the American West, which had been receiving settlers since the Louisiana Purchase of 1803 (under then President Thomas Jefferson). American's movement west, under the premise of manifest destiny, brought out the best and worst in America. The belief was that out west was where dreams could be made (and with the Gold Rush of 1849, where riches could be found). This was the principle that originally brought settlers to the Americas, and it was in this idea that part of America culture, that a better life was available, was made. Expansion west, though, also brought with it war and suffering (both an official war with Mexico and unofficial ones against the American Indians), as well as bringing the North and South into conflict over the expansion of slavery. This disagreement of what to do with the lands out west (whether to allow them to be slave or free) precipitated the American Civil War.

The transcontinental railroad is one of America's crowing achievements of the 19th century, on par with the building of the Erie Canal. It was a vital link for the American West for trade, travel and commerce. The line provided a safer and quicker way for Americans to head out west over land (replacing the slower and more dangerous stagecoach lines and wagon trains that had preceded it). Construction of the railroad helped settle the west, as the railroad sold land-grant lots along its route. The ease of transport brought with it timber and crops from the east, allowing for the creation of homes, businesses, towns and cities.

The building of the lines brought together American capitalism with immigrant labor. Those who worked on the railroad were both Army veterans and Irish and Chinese immigrants. Army veterans who had experience keeping trains running during the Civil War made up the engineers for the route. The Central Pacific, unable to draw from the same labor pool and facing shortages in their own force in the West, utilized Irish and Chinese immigrants.

Building of the line was impacted by political forces and corporate greed. Originally, the route the line was to take fell prey to the problems the country was experiencing between North and South. With Southern secession, the main opposition to a central route for the Transcontinental Route disappeared. However, the line was still not free from outside political forces, namely the constraints of trying to construct a major project during a war. While the Central Pacific was able to begin construction in 1863, the Union Pacific Railroad, which would have started its construction tens of miles away from where the fighting was going on, did not start its route in earnest until July 1865. Unfortunately for America, the war was only part of the problem with the Union Pacific. Inept oversight and greedy managers at Union Pacific also contributed to the slow progress initially for the company.

The building of the line also improved communication for America. Needing the ability to communicate with its workers, the railroad companies laid telegraph lines as they were building the tracks. This telegraph line was both easier to protect and easier to maintain than the First Transcontinental Telegraph lines, whose route followed the Mormon Trail and Central Nevada Route. In fact, the telegraph laid down for the Transcontinental Railroad eventually superseded these older lines, and the original Transcontinental Telegraph lines were eventually abandoned.

The work involved was tremendous, as was the area covered. The Union Pacific laid down 1,087 miles of track. They began in Council Bluffs, followed the Missouri River through Nebraska, the Colorado Territory, the Wyoming Territory and the Utah Territory. The Central Pacific laid fewer tracks (690 miles) but in some regards had a harder go of it. They began in Sacramento, California and continued over the Sierra Nevada Mountains. Work in the mountains was both slow and dangerous, as the company needed to literally blast its way through. Getting through the mountains, the company then took the line through Nevada and connected up with the Union Pacific at Promontory Summit in the Utah Territory. The path follows modern-day interstate 80.

While the line connected the west and the east, the route chosen was not ideal. The original line did not pass through either Denver or Salt Lake City, which represented the two largest cities in the west. Lines were eventually built to connect these two great cities of the Great American Desert (as the West was sometimes called) with the Transcontinental Railroad.

Just as interesting, the original line of the Union Pacific did not connect into the Eastern US rail network. Initially to get a train from America's east coast to its west's, a ferry had to be used to connect the train from America's eastern network of rails into the Transcontinental Railroad across the Missouri River. This kink was worked out in 1873, when the Union Pacific built and opened the Missouri River Bridge.

The history, trial and tribulations of building the Transcontinental Railroad encompassed everything that 19th century America was experiencing: the politics of slavery; the expansion out into the west; emerging capitalism and laissez-fair government (along with the abuses of each); immigrant workers; and the American Civil War.

Chapter 1: History

Dreams of a transcontinental railroad started in 1830 with the advent of the steam powered railroads in Great Britain. When they were introduced to America, the belief was that America would eventually build a route that would connect her eastern ocean (the Atlantic) with its assumed western one (the Pacific, for America did not technically own any territory that connected with that ocean at the time). With improvements in railroad technology, as well as the territories that America added through purchase (Oregon) and war (California), the hope was that the transcontinental railroad would be built soon. It is important to note that there never was a debate about whether the line would be built. What would fall prey to politics for the Transcontinental Railroad was what direction it would go (what route it would follow) and how would it be paid for.

The route was what concerned the US government the most. Those who favored a central route did so to avoid the worst passes of the Rocky Mountains. Such a route would follow the Platte River in Nebraska and the South Pass through the Rocky Mountains in Wyoming, following the path of the Oregon Trail. Others favored a southern route, which would avoid the Rocky Mountains altogether. The route would take passengers across Texas, through New Mexico, across the Sonoro desert and into

Los Angeles California. Finally, there was the northern route, which was similar to the route followed by the Lewis and Clark Expedition. This route would go along the Missouri River through present-day northern Montana to Oregon Territory. This route, though, was considered undesirable due to the high amount of snow expected along this path.

Champion of the Central Route

One of the foremost advocates for a central route for the Transcontinental Railroad was Asa Whitney. Whitney, who was a distant cousin of the cotton gin inventor Eli Whitney, wanted a route that went from Chicago and the Great Lakes area into Northern California. To pay for the railroad, he was in favor of selling land along the route to settlers.

In 1845, Whitney accompanied a team along the proposed route to assess whether or not it was plausible. During this travel, Whitney solicited support from businessmen and politicians. Asa printed maps and pamphlets and submitted several proposals of the desired route to Congress. He paid for all this work himself. Congress responded with the writing of legislation to begin construction of the Pacific Railroad. While it was introduced to Congress by Representative Zadock Pratt, Congress did not act on any of Whitney's proposals, and so the plan never got off the ground.

Part of Congress's reluctance had to do with the land in question. In 1845, the boundaries of Oregon were not resolved and California was not part of the US. The Oregon boundary was a contentious issue between America and Great Britain. As for California, the US was embroiled in the Mexican War at the time. As such, both lands were not US possessions.

. All of that changed in 1846. In that year, the Oregon Question was settled when the United States and Great Britain agreed on the 49th parallel as the border for the United States and Canada in Oregon. Later on in that same year US forces took over California. Two years later California came under formal US control with the Treaty of Guadalupe Hidalgo, which officially ended the Mexican-American War. The discovery of gold in California in January 1848 set off the California Gold Rush, which swelled California's population over night (allowing it to become the 31st state just two years later).

A Southern Route

With the acquisition of the land, it seemed that Whitney's proposed route was within reach. Still, Congress and developers worried about the snow in and around the Rocky Mountains, and many felt that a central route to California simply did not make sense because of this. In 1848, Congress ordered its own survey done. The results showed that the best route for the Transcontinental Railroad was a southern one. The problem was that parts of this ideal route still belonged to Mexico.

To settle this, the US in 1853 made the Gadsden Purchase. In this purchase, Mexico agreed to sell the southern portions of what is now New Mexico and Arizona to the United States. The cost for America was $5,000,000 (somewhat disconcerting, for if the survey had been done earlier the US could have demanded the land as part of the peace treaty that ended the Mexican War). Nevertheless, the route for the Transcontinental Railroad was now supposedly clear. It would be south, and it would be built (with the Gadsden Purchase) now entirely within U.S. territory.

Or so it would seem. The politics of the day, and the issues of slavery, made Congress unable to act. As America was divided between slave and non-slave state members, Congress at the time could not reach any agreement on any route.

Each side would argue for a particular route, with the benefits that would come to each. The decision on the route became caught up in the sectional disputes associated with slavery (issues that would lead to the American Civil War). The southern route was abandoned (and no construction would be done along this proposed route until 1880, when the Southern Pacific Railroad built a lone route across Arizona).

Chapter 2: Theodore Judah

With the southern route in limbo, the door was wide open for the central route to be reconsidered. Taking up this cause was Theodore Judah. After surveying the route Judah began working on a plan to overcome the largest obstacle of the central route: a way to construct it over the high and rugged Sierra Nevada Mountains.

Judah came in with credibility. He was chief engineer for the Sacramento Valley Railroad. In 1852, that the company built the first railroad that was west of the Mississippi River. The fact that this company would later fail did not deter Judah and his ambitions.

Judah was convinced that a railroad could pass from the East through the Great Basin, over the Sierra Nevada Mountains and onto Sacramento. In 1856, Judah wrote a 13,000 word proposal calling for such a railroad. The proposal was sent to the United States Cabinet, Congress, and other influential people of the time. Three years later, Judah was chosen to be the lobbyist for the Pacific Railroad Convention. Looking at his proposal, the convention approved Judah's plan to survey, finance and engineer a central route for the Transcontinental Railroad. At the end, of 1859 Judah returned back to Washington DC, where he had an audience with the President. He also represented the Pacific Railroad

Convention and their interest before a meeting of Congress.

His efforts were partially successful. In February of 1860, Iowa Representative Samuel Curtis introduced a bill in the House of Representative to build the railroad that was identical to the proposal put forth by Judah. The measure passed in the House. The Senate, though, modified the proposal. When the House and Senate could not reconcile the bill, the proposal died.

With that defeat, Judah returned to California, hoping to find investors to fund the route. On one of his speaking engagements for a Transcontinental Railroad, he caught the attention of Collis Huntington, a hardware merchant. Huntington met with Judah after his presentation in Sacramento. He invited Judah to his office to hear his proposal in detail. Originally Judah hoped to raise funds from several investors. Huntington changed Judah's mind, and pushed him towards finding the money for the route from four partners: Mark Hopkins, Huntington's business partner; James Bailey, a jeweler; Leland Stanford, a grocer, future governor of California, and founder of Stanford University; and Charles Crocker, a dry-goods merchant and eventual owner of Crocker Banks. Judah eventually agreed, though in time

he would regret it. The four at first invested
$1,500 each and formed a board of directors.
Hopkins, Bailey, Stanford and Crocker
eventually became known as the Big Four, and
the investment they made became the railroad
company called the Central Pacific Railroad. The
investment would pay each handsomely (in
millions of dollars).

Chapter 3: Getting through the Sierra Mountains

With the financial backing, of the Big Four Judah began to search for a more practical route through the Sierras. In the summer of 1860, he found his answer from a local miner. Daniel Strong, who was surveying a route through the Sierras for a wagon toll road, found one that would suit a railroad. He sent a letter to Judah notifying him of such. Judah formed an association with Strong that would solicit subscriptions from local merchants and businessmen to the proposed route.

In 1861 Judah and Strong led a ten person team on an expedition. They surveyed the Sierra Nevada passage that Strong had discovered, a passage that went through Clipper Gap, Emigrant Gap, Donner Pass and onward south to Truckee. The path they discovered had a gradual incline to allow for a train to pass through.

Judah hoped that this passage would convince Congress to change its mind about a central passage for the Transcontinental Railroad. He also hoped it to provide the impetus to find funds to buy out the Big Four (an association he was never entirely comfortable with). He traveled back to New York City to do as much. Shortly after arriving, however, Judah came down with yellow fever (contracted while working on the Panama Railroad). He died on

November 2, 1863. The Central Pacific Railroad (CPRR) soon appointed Samuel Montegue to succeed Judah as its Chief Engineer (with Lewis Metzler Clement becoming Chief Assistant Engineer and Superintendent of Track).

Chapter 4: Pacific Railroad Act

The Pony Express, which carried US mail, showed that the Central Nevada Route, the one that Judah had surveyed and that stretched across Nevada and Utah along the Oregon Trail and across Wyoming and Nebraska, was a viable route, even in the winter. With this realization, one of the main obstacles to a central path (concern about the snow) was removed. Politics and war would remove a second. The American Civil War was soon to take with it the dissent of the southern states of the central route (as they would secede and hence no longer be part of the Union or Congress). Furthermore, a secessionist movement was gaining steam in California. To keep it part of the Union, it needed to be connected to the rest of America. To do that a railroad was needed.

1862 again saw the introduction of a bill by Curtis in the House of Representatives. The bill called for the establishment of a railroad into the American West. It was almost identical to the one put forward years before. With the secession, of the southern states opposition to Curtis's bill dissipated. On May 6, 1862, the bill passed in the House of Representatives. A month later, on June 20, the bill finally was approved by the Senate. On July 1st, President Lincoln signed the bill into law.

The Pacific Railroad Act established two main

lines to connect the Eastern part of America with the West. The Central Pacific was established from the west. From the Midwest, the Union Pacific line was established. Other rail lines were encouraged to connect into these two main lines with feeder lines.

The bill laid forth a timeline and expectation for both companies. Both the Central Pacific and Union Pacific were required to build 50 miles of track each year. Payments were made on track laid and based on the grade of the ground. The railroads would receive $16,000 for each mile they laid over easy grade (flat land). For track laid in the high plains, the companies would receive $32,000 per mile of track. For the most difficult part of the route, (the mountains, especially the Rocky and Sierra Mountains) the companies would be compensated $48,000 for each mile of track laid. Payment was not in money but instead in the form of government bonds. The companies were able to turn around and sell these bonds to others.

The US government realized, though, that other monies would be needed. Congress provided land grants of federal lands in the West to the railroad companies as an additional form of compensation. The land was tied to the track that was being laid. The companies were granted right-of-ways of 400 feet plus ten square miles of land next to the track for each mile of track they lay. To avoid a railroad monopoly on the good land (land along the route), the companies did not receive one large continuous swath of land on one side of the track or the other but rather a checkerboard pattern. They would receive land on either side of the track, with government-owned land in between the land grants. This federal land could be purchased from the government (ostensibly to be sold to others beside the railroad companies).

This compensation package created a competition between the Central Pacific and Union Pacific. The more tracks the company laid meant more money and land the company would receive. But there was a finite amount, as the more tracks the other company laid meant less track that they could lay.

All in all, the Railroad Act granted a large amount of the area to both companies. The total amount of land granted to the Union Pacific and Central Pacific railroad companies, between federal and state land grants, was about 7,244,000,000 square meters. To put this in perspective, this is more land area than what makes up the state of Texas.

Many argued at the time that the compensation the companies received (land and government bonds) was actually a government subsidy for what was to become a privately run business. Since the companies repaid both the capital and interest, others argue that it could not be considered a subsidy. It is also important to understand what the compensation actually meant. While both railroad companies received a lot of land, it was not all beachfront property. The companies were able to earn money on the sale of the land in the Sacramento Valley and Nebraska. The compensation it received in terms of lands in Wyoming, Utah and Nevada, though, was far less, as this land was unable to be sold and as such became worthless.

Selection of the Eastern Terminus

With the selection of the central route part of the Transcontinental Railroad intrigue was laid to rest. The path through the West was determined. With a central path the western terminus was also easily determined (as it would be Sacramento). Where the eastern terminus would be (and thus, where it would eventually tie into the rest of America), though, was still up for debate. The Pacific Railroad Act only specified who was to win the contract for the work from the East. It did not specify where the Eastern Terminus was to be. The Act left that decision up to President Lincoln to formally choose the location for the railroad to start in the East.

At the passage of the Pacific Railroad Act there were three possible candidates for the Eastern Terminus. The first was Council Bluffs / Omaha, a terminus proposed by Thomas Durant through an extension of his proposed Mississippi and Missouri Railroad via the new Union Pacific Railroad. The second was at St. Joseph, Missouri via the Hannibal and St. Joseph Railroad (H&SJ). Finally, the last possible place for the Western Terminus was at Kansas City, , Kansas via the Leavenworth, Pawnee and Western Railroad (LP&W) (later called the Kansas Pacific). This line was initially controlled by Thomas Ewing, Jr. and later by John C. Fremont.

While each had its own advantages, two

terminuses stuck out: Council Bluffs and St. Joseph. Council Bluffs was well north of the war raging on in the South (the Civil War was having many battles in Missouri). This area also offered the shortest route to the South Pass break in the Rockies in Wyoming. Finally, this short route to the west followed a fertile river, which would encourage settlement along the route.

St. Joseph Missouri had its advantages, as well. It had the only railroad that actually reached the Missouri River on its western border (and thus could tie in to the rest of the Eastern seaboard). St. Joseph was more centrally located (especially for those lines coming up from Texas; once it rejoined the Union, of course). St. Joseph Missouri could also offer a route that would service Denver, Colorado, what was then the biggest city in the Great American Desert. At the passage of the Pacific Railroad Act, the closest rail lines to Omaha / Council Bluffs were about 150 miles away. They would not reach Omaha for another five years (in 1867).

Chapter 5: A Decision is Made

As with most things, what was offered was not nearly as important as whom you knew. And in the choice of the Eastern Terminus, the Council Bluffs / Omaha location knew some pretty influential people.

Thomas Durant, a man who was building the cross-Iowa railroad (the M&M), banked on the fact that the Eastern Terminus would be at Omaha. He put his money where his beliefs were, buying up land in Nebraska that would connect to this Terminus. He had good reason to be so confident.

In 1857, Durant hired then-private citizen Abraham Lincoln as an attorney to represent the M&M. The case involved steamboat operators who hoped to dismantle Government Bridge, the first bridge across the Mississippi River. While important for land travel, the bridge prevented steamboats from passing underneath it. As such, it was an obstruction of a public waterway. While arguing for the M&M Company, Lincoln was first introduced to Council Bluffs.

In August 1859 Lincoln, now on his way to the running for the Presidency and at the behest of M&M attorney Norman Judd, again traveled to Council Bluffs to inspect M&M facilities that were to be used to secure a $3,000 loan, a loan that Lincoln himself was to hold. During the visit, Lincoln rode the SJ&H railroad, which took him into Missouri and Kansas before reaching Council Bluffs. It was during this time that Lincoln spent 2 hours with M&M engineer Grenville M. Dodge at the Pacific House Hotel, where Dodge told the future President of the advantages of having the Eastern Terminus in Council Bluffs. Lincoln even visited Cemetery Hill, where he was shown the proposed route from Omaha.

Lincoln's ties to Council Bluffs / Omaha were strengthened by what had occurred during the 1860 Republican Convention. A hotly contested affair, Lincoln was able to secure the Republic nomination on the convention's third ballot when the Iowa delegation switched its votes and backed him. Missouri (where St. Joseph, the other possible site of the Eastern Terminus, was located) only gave Lincoln 10 percent of the vote in the 1860 Presidential Election.

With such ties and political backing, the decision on the Eastern Terminus came rather easily to Lincoln. In 1862, he followed the advice of his former client and chose Council Bluffs / Omaha as the Eastern Terminus for the Transcontinental Railroad.

While they did not receive the decision they wanted, both the H&SJ and LP&W were not totally shut out of the contract. The H&SJ was allowed to build a feeder line from Atchison, Kansas, while the LP&W could build a feeder line out of Kansas City, Kansas. The plan was for these lines to meet the main line of the Union Pacific somewhere around the 100th meridian west in central Nebraska. Both the H&SJ and the LP&W would also receive the same land grant incentives as the Union Pacific.

The Union Pacific Line

Almost immediately, the Union Pacific line arrangements ran into trouble. The company that would eventually build two-thirds of the Transcontinental Railroad suffered through controversy and scandals while its controlling partner, Thomas Durant, got rich. This was due to lax government oversight, as well as the problems that the Union faced in dealing with its Civil War (this was in contrast with what was going on in the West. Practically unaffected by the Civil War, the Central Pacific was able to proceed ahead with rather straightforward arrangements).

There were concerns about building the track while the war raged. While no battles came close to the proposed line, there were thoughts that the Union would need to protect it when it was built. Those in the North also constantly worried about sabotage. Disrupting a route to the West seemed like a likely Southern war aim.

Another part of the problem was in the Pacific Railroad Act itself. The legislation required that no partner in the Union Pacific own more than 10 percent of the stock of the company. The Union Pacific, however, was having issues selling its stock. To overcome this, Durant came up with a scheme. He would put up the money to investors for the stock, with the investors putting their name on the sale. Thus, Durant was able to gain control of nearly half of the company, which was against Congress's wishes.

Further issues occurred because of the route of the line. The initial construction from the east went over land that Durant had purchased. To milk the federal government, Durant had extraneous tracks built in the area. Over the first two and a half years of work, the track did not stretch further then 40 miles past Omaha.

Durant also manipulated the price of the stock market for his own gains. He would spread rumors about which railroads were to be connected to the Union Pacific. He first let it be known that his M&M line would feed into it (thus driving up the value of his stock) while he secretly bought up the stock of the Cedar Rapids and Missouri Railroad (CR&M, whose stock was nose diving as investors believed that it would not be connected to the Transcontinental Railroad). Durant then ran up CR&M stocks when he announced new plans to connect it with the Union Pacific Line (and he made a lot of profit selling those stocks he bought at reduced prices). Durant then took those earning and he, along with his associates, began buying M&M stocks as its price began to plummet. Then the pattern would repeat itself. It is estimated that these stock manipulations netted Durant and his friends some $5 million.

Durant was able to get away with this because he kept a low profile. He only acted as vice president of the Union Pacific, and used the cover of respected men serving as president of the company (John Adams Dix, for one).

With the end of the Civil War, came more focus on the Transcontinental Railroad. The fact that the Union Pacific had only gotten 40 miles outside of Omaha (in two and a half years) brought with it increase government scrutiny. Durant hired his former M&M engineer Grenville M. Dodge to build the railroad. The Union Pacific began a mad dash to make up for the time Durant had wasted.

Chapter 6: Construction

As noted, the Pacific Railroad Act required that each company lay 50 miles worth of track a year. To handle that workload, which at times could be very dangerous, immigrants were used. The majority of the work done at Union Pacific was done by Irish laborers and, after the end of the Civil War, veterans of both the Union and Confederate armies.

But others were utilized along the way. Brigham Young, founder of the Mormon Church, hoped to have the railroads encourage emigration of the populace to Ogden and Salt Lake City, Utah. As the Union Pacific approached Utah Territory, Young sought a labor contract with the Union Pacific. As part of the contract, nearly all of the work the company engaged in the Utah Area was done by Mormons. This included the extensive blasting and tunneling through the Weber River canyon.

For the Central Pacific, most of the work was done by Chinese immigrants. At first this was not a popular decision, as they were thought too fragile to perform the tough work required of them. After several days, that opinion was quickly overturned. The company saw the good work the workers were performing and decided to try to hire as many Chinese workers as could be found in California (many were there due to the gold rush, either as independent miners or working in such service industries in the area such as laundries and kitchens). Many more Chinese workers were imported directly from China. The Chinese immigrants received between one and three dollars of pay per day. The workers imported from China were not compensated as much. This led to discord in the ranks, and the workers directly from China went on strike. Eventually, they received a small increase in their pay.

A large part of the work consisted of laying down the tracks. The work was broken up into various parts, each headed up by a different group (or work gang). One gang would lay down the ties (the wooden planks). Another would lay the rails onto those ties. A third gang would drive the spikes and bolt the splice bars. A fourth gang, at the same time, would distribute telegraph poles and wire along the route. The workers did not employ any machines in their endeavors, so almost all of the work was done manually. Workers used shovels to dig, picks and axes to break up rock. Black powder was used where manual labor could not create a pass. Dirt and rocks were carted out on two-wheeled dump carts and wheelbarrows. The closest thing to machines the workers had were mules and horses, which would drag away the heavier materials (as well as bring in the needed supplies). Supply trains would ride along the newly laid tracks to bring in all the necessary material for the rail construction, which consisted of ties, rails, spikes, bolts, telegraph poles, and wire.

The workers became a moving community. As such the railroad companies had to employ service workers. For example, cooks were brought in to travel with the men and prepare meals every day for the workers. The company would also employ clerks and secretaries who would keep track of supplies, accounts and records and who would use the telegraph wire freshly lay to report back on progress, as well as to make requests for more materials and supplies

Track laying took up about 25% of the labor force employed in building the Transcontinental Railroad. Laying the track, as it turned out, was the easy part. Creating the path required the work of others, specialists in the field. Over the course of its construction, the Transcontinental Railroad employed hundreds of tunnelers, explosive experts, bridge builders, blacksmiths, carpenters, engineers, masons, and surveyors.

Central Pacific Line

On January 8, 1863, at a ceremony in Sacramento, California, Governor Leland Stanford broke ground to officially begin the construction of the Central Pacific Railroad. The work proceeded quickly in the Sacramento Valley, and the Central Pacific seemed to be ahead of schedule. When the company came to the foothills of the Sierra Nevada, though, the pace slowed down considerably. The mountains proved to be an issue. So too did the winter that brought with it dangerous snow storms.

To combat this, and to maintain the required pace of 50 miles of track per year, the Central Pacific Railroad began hiring more and more immigrant workers. These workers, desperate for any job, as such were more willing to work in the horrible conditions that the company was now presented with. The need for tunneling through the mountains, though, worked to slow the progress again of the now swelled workforce of the Central Pacific.

Tunneling

This slowdown in progress was due to the slow pace of tunneling through the mountains. At the time tunneling was done through blasting. The companies used black powder and for the Summit Tunnel nitroglycerin to blast through the granite slopes. To carve a tunnel was a dangerous job. One worker would hold a rock drill on the granite of the mountain while two other workers would swing eighteen pound sledgehammers to chisel a hole in the rock. The black powder was then placed in the hole, and one worker would be asked to light the fuse. Many died from these explosions, either in the initial blast, the falling debris from the explosion, or by snow slides and avalanches caused by the explosion.

For the tunnel blasting through the Sierra Nevada Mountains, the Chinese were used. In all Chinese immigrants built 15 tunnels for Central Pacific. The longest was the summit tunnel, which stretched 1,659 feet. Each of the tunnels would be about 32 feet high and about 16 feet wide. Loose rocks were first removed with derricks, though a machine powered by steam eventually replaced them.

Progress in tunneling was slow work. The Central Pacific averaged around a foot of progress through the mountains a day while they were tunneling. The workers during this part of the construction worked three shifts of 8 hour shifts. They were overseen by two foremen, working 12 hour shifts.

Union Pacific

As described previously, work on the Union Pacific side of the Transcontinental Railroad was slow in getting off the ground. This was due to events beyond the company's control (the Civil War) and events very much under their control (corruption by Durant). In time Grenville Dodge was appointed to oversee the Union Pacific's construction efforts.

Work began at the Eastern Terminus, at Omaha, Nebraska. When the work was done in earnest (and not subject to Durant's corruption), the company moved along very quickly in the open terrain of the Great Plains. When the work entered Indian-held land, however, the work slowed. The Native Americans viewed the railroad with contempt and saw it as a violation of the many treaties they had signed with the United States. Indian war parties began to harass the labor camps of the Union Pacific. In response, the Union Pacific added security to the labor camps. It also began hiring marksmen to kill American Bison. The Bison, a physical threat to the trains, also served as a primary source of food for many of the Native Americans. This only intensified the issue. Seeing the "Iron Horse" (as the train was known to the Native Americans) as a threat to their very existence, the Indians began killing Union Pacific laborers.

The cycle of violence intensified. Union Pacific

added further security measures, and an undeclared war broke out between the Native Americans and the Union Pacific. The violence only grew, which led the death toll to rise for both sides. Despite their efforts, though, the Native Americans could not prevent the advances of the Union Pacific. The progress on the railroad continued.

Sabotage

Because of the nature of the contract awarded to Union Pacific and Central Pacific, with payments made for the amount of track laid, the two companies were given to sabotage one another. They would steal supplies, detonate each other's black powder, all with the hope of claiming more land (and more track) as their own. When they first came close to meeting, both companies changed paths to be nearly parallel, so that each company could claim payment from the government over the same plot of land.

Near Completion

Fed up with this fighting and sabotage, and wanting to see the job finally completed, Congress eventually declared where and when the railways should meet. The government sent out survey teams to closely follow the work crews of both the Union Pacific and the Central Pacific. This had the desired result, as each now raced to the aforementioned finish line. It also led to some pretty amazing work. A leading Central Pacific road crew set a record for the time by laying 10 miles of track in a single day. They commemorated the event by posting a signpost alongside the track for passing trains to see.

The Final Spike

In 1869, six years after work initially began, the railroad from the east finally met the railroad from the west. As designated by Congress, the Central Pacific Railroad and its workers (and line) met up with the Union Pacific Railroad (along with its workers and line) at Promontory Summit, in Utah. For the event, on May 10, 1869, four ceremonial spikes were driven to signify the completion of the work. The last of these spikes, the golden spike, was driven in by Stanford.

The completion of the line was a media frenzy for the country. In perhaps what could be called the world's first live mass-media event, the hammers and spike were wired to the telegraph line that ran along the train line. Each hammer stroke would be heard as a click at telegraph stations nationwide. This "live" event, though, did have some problems, as some of the hammer strokes were missed by the telegraph (and so had to be sent as clicks by the telegraph operator). When the ceremonial spike was replaced with an ordinary spike (and was sent to Cantor Arts Center at Stanford University for display), a message was transmitted over the newly laid telegraph to both the East and West Coast of America. The message simply said "Done". With that, the country rejoiced. Travel overland from the Eastern Coast of America to the Western Coast (and vice versa) was reduced from six months or more to just one week.

Chapter 7: Railroad Developments

Of course, the east and west coast was not officially connected, at least not yet. The Transcontinental Railroad only connected Omaha to Sacramento. Omaha still was not tied into the rest of the Eastern coast network of trains. And Sacramento was not even connected to the rest of California. It took until November 1869 before the Central Pacific finally connected Sacramento to San Francisco Bay at Oakland, California. The Union Pacific would not connect Omaha to Council Bluffs until completing the Union Pacific Missouri River Bridge in 1873.

Troubles also were brewing with the central route that the train had taken. The Central Pacific realized early on the trouble it would have in keeping the track open across the Sierras in the winter months. The company first tried plowing the track with specially designed snowplows that were mounted on steam engines. When this failed to produce a satisfactory solution the company took to building snow sheds over some of the track. This helped keep these areas free from snow for all but a few days of the year.

Both companies realized that they needed to upgrade their bridges, viaducts, and dug ways, as well as utilize heavier duty rails, stronger ties and better road beds. Originally speed had been the concern of the company. They attempted to lay down the track as quickly as possible. Maintenance and longevity were secondary issues. With the track now done, both companies now paid attention to such matters.

When the West and East Actually Connected

With the end of the Civil War, competing railroads of the Union Pacific coming in from Missouri took advantage. A building boom ensued. The H&SJ constructed the Hannibal Bridge, the first bridge to cross the Missouri River, in July 1869 in Kansas City. Denver Pacific Railway built a feeder line into the Union Pacific. In August 1870, the Kansas Pacific laid the last spike connecting to the Denver Pacific line at Strasburg, Colorado. This represented the first true connection of the Atlantic to the Pacific by railroad for the United States.

On June 4, 1876, an express train called the Transcontinental Express arrived in San Francisco after having traveled over the First Transcontinental Railroad. It had departed from New York City, and in only 83 hours and 39 minutes, it found itself on the west coast. Coast to coast travel over land had officially begun.

Trouble at Union Pacific

Despite the success the Transcontinental Railroad brought to the company, the Union Pacific faced bankruptcy less than three years after the golden spike was driven in. The problem had to do with overcharges Credit Mobilier had billed Union Pacific for the formal building of the railroad. The scandal over these charged hit epic proportions in the United States presidential election of 1872. It would be looked at as one of the largest scandals of America's Gilded Age, and it would not be resolved for several more years.

Not surprisingly, in the middle of this scandal was Durant. Durant had initially come up with a scheme where Union Pacific would subcontract the actual track work of building the Transcontinental Railroad to a company called Credit Mobilier. Durant in turn gained control of the Credit Mobilier Company when he bought out employee Herbert Hoxie for $10,000. Under Durant's guidance, the company was charging Union Pacific two to three times more the customary price for the work being performed. Durant did not mind, as he was in fact, paying himself, though the scheme did slow down the Union Pacific work.

To rectify the situation, President Lincoln turned to Massachusetts Congressman Oakes Ames. Ames, who was on the Congressional Railroad

Committee, was charged with getting things moving and cleaning up the situation. Instead, he only muddied things up even more. Ames had his brother Oliver Ames, Jr. named president of the Union Pacific. Ames in turn became president of Credit Mobilier.

To avoid Congressional oversight, Ames began paying off members of Congress. He granted these politicians and others stock options in his company. Politicians who allegedly received such options were Vice President Schuyler Colfax (who was cleared) and future President James Garfield, among others. Ames also continued to gauge Union Pacific.

Years later, the scandal broke. In 1872, the New York Sun published letters and correspondence between Henry McComb and Ames detailing the scheme. The ensuing Congressional investigation resulted in the censure of Ames (although there were those who wanted Ames expelled from Congress). This all became moot, as Ames died within three months of the scandal breaking.

By the time the scandal hit, Durant had left the Union Pacific. In his place came Jay Gould. Gould took advantage of the stock market panic of 1873 to pick up good bargains. Two of those bargains became controlling interest of the

Union Pacific Railroad and Western Union.

Central Pacific

The Central Pacific did not enjoy sustained success either. In 1885, the company was absorbed by Southern Pacific. Sixteen years later, Union Pacific attempted to take over Southern Pacific through purchase of its stock. The US Supreme Court felt that this would give Union Pacific a monopoly on the transcontinental railroad and forced Union Pacific to divest from the company. Ninety five years later, in 1996, Union Pacific eventually did complete its takeover of Southern Pacific.

Later Developments for Promontory Summit

Improvements were constantly made both to the track itself and to the route it took. In 1904 Lucin Cutoff was seen as a better route to travel then across Promontory Summit, and so the route was diverted through there. In 1942, the Promontory Summit rails were pulled, as they were recycled for the World War II effort.

As there had been a ceremony for the driving of the last spike, so too was there a ceremony for the "undriving" of the spikes. In 1957, Congress authorized the Golden Spike National Historic Site at Promontory Summit, to commemorate the importance of the area. On May 10, 2006, on the anniversary of the driving of the spike, the state of Utah announced that its state quarter design would be a representation of the driving of the golden spike.

Visible Remains of the Railroad

With the advent of airplanes and cars, the Transcontinental Railroad fell into disuse. Several of the lines were bypassed and abandoned. Still, remnants of the line remain. In Utah, the road grades of the Transcontinental Railroad are obvious, as are some of the numerous cuts and fills done for it.

Hundreds of miles of the historic line are still in service as well, sometimes on part original to the rail line. Amtrak's California Zephyr, a daily passenger service from Emeryville, California (San Francisco Bay Area) to Chicago, still uses the First Transcontinental Railroad line from Sacramento to central Nevada. While the original rail has been replaced (due to the age and wear of the rail), and the roadbed of the track has been upgraded and repaired, the lines of today generally run on top of the original, handmade grade.

Chapter 8: Conclusion

Popular Culture

The experiences of building the Transcontinental Railroad inspired millions, becoming the basis of many a story, both about the construction itself and about the ideas it conjured in the mind. The joining together at Promontory Summit, Utah of the Union Pacific line with the Central Pacific was one of the major inspirations for French writer Jules Verne's book entitled Around the World in Eighty Days, which was published four years after the event in the year 1873.

With the advent of movies the work done on the Transcontinental Railroad became a source for several stories. The construction is depicted in various movies, including the 1939 film Union Pacific, starring Joel McCrea and Barbara Stanwyck and directed by Cecil B. DeMille. John Ford's 1924 silent movie The Iron Horse captures the fervent nationalism that drove public support for the project. Ironically, several of the actors portraying cooks were some of the Chinese laborers who actually worked on the Central Pacific section of the railroad. The 1962 film How the West Was Won has a whole segment devoted to the construction, including a famous scene of a buffalo stampede over the railroad.

Even today, the importance of the construction is relevant. The main character in The Claim, a 2000 feature film, is a surveyor for the Central

Pacific Railroad, and the film's focus in part is about the efforts of a frontier mayor to have part of the Transcontinental Railroad run through his town.

The lore of the construction, though, is not regulated only to the movies. The children's book Ten Mile Day by Mary Ann Fraser tells the story of the final, record setting push by the Central Pacific when they laid down 10 miles of track in a single day. The event, occurring on April 28, 1869, was done (in the book at least) to settle a $10,000 bet. Kristiana Gregory's book The Great Railroad Race is written as a diary by Libby West, whose writings chronicle the end of the building of the line and the enthusiasm which overwhelmed the country at the news.

In TV, the series American Experience documented the railway in the episode titled "Transcontinental Railroad". The building of the railway is covered by the 2004 BBC documentary series Seven Wonders of the Industrial World in episode 6, "The Line". Even the popular British Show Doctor Who featured the Transcontinental Railroad in a BBC audio book.

Legacy of the Transcontinental Railroad

The importance of the Transcontinental Railroad lays in its rich and storied history. Its creation was tied to the politics of the days. While seen as needed as early as 1830, it took nearly forty years to build because of the problems inherent not in the concept of the line but in America itself (as the route of the train became embroiled in the fight between the North and the South). Initially it helped serve the North in its Civil War efforts. At the War's end, it paved the way for Western expansion, making it affordable and safe for Americans to travel out west. During its construction, it helped build the fortune of many a men (sometimes legally, other times unethically). The Transcontinental Railroad allowed for a quicker settlement of America's West.

With the rise of automobiles and air travel, its importance dwindled. During the war efforts of the Second World War, it was pulled apart for materials. Still, the memory of the railroad lives on. We see remnants of it. We hear stories of about it. America is the country it is today because of it. In that the legacy of the Transcontinental Railroad will live on.

Made in the USA
Lexington, KY
02 September 2012